Find it! Explore it!

NATIONAL GEOGRAPHIC KiDS

Ocean

READY TO DIVE INTO AWESOME UNDERWATER WORLDS?

Here's how it works!

On the FIND IT! pages, search the image for the creatures shown at the bottom of the page. The number next to each animal's name tells you how many are hidden in the scene!

Exploring **TIDE POOLS**

Tide pools are pockets of water that are left behind on beaches when the tide goes out. Creatures like crabs and lobsters have adapted to life on land and in shallow water because of tide pools.

Did you know?
The force of gravity from the sun and moon creates tides.

Find it!

1 Lobster   2 Gobies   3 Oystercatchers   4 Hermit crabs   5 Whelks   6 Urchins   7 Sea stars   8 Crabs

HERMIT CRAB

Hermit crabs are not actually crabs; they cannot form their own shells. Instead, they borrow shells from other animals—like whelks and other sea snails—or anything they can get their pincers on!

One type of hermit crab is all right-handed, and another is all left-handed. Try writing your name with the hand you don't usually use.

COMMON CUTTLEFISH can control how they float and what color they are. Baby cuttlefish use their tentacles to walk along the seafloor!

Explore it!

OYSTERCATCHER
Oystercatchers have long colorful beaks, which they use to open shellfish. They have white markings on their wings, which make them pretty easy to spot.

GOBY
Gobies are a type of small fish. In some species, when the female lays eggs, the male guards them very closely.

LOBSTER
Lobsters have long tails and big claws. They never stop growing. Lobsters are known for having long lives, with some species living for over 100 years.

Can you rearrange the letters below to make the name of another animal with claws?
B R A C

Then, on the EXPLORE IT! pages, you'll learn all about the animals you just found.

NATIONAL GEOGRAPHIC
Washington, D.C.

The Precious
PACIFIC OCEAN

The Pacific Ocean is the biggest ocean in the world. The Great Barrier Reef is found here. It is the world's largest reef, and it is packed with many animals such as fish, sea turtles, and seahorses as well as lots of colorful coral.

1 Pufferfish

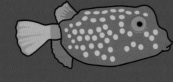

2 Boxfish

3 Lionfish

4 Parrotfish

Find it! 🔍

5 Porcupine-fish

6 Surgeonfish

7 Anemones

8 Clownfish

CLOWNFISH AND SEA ANEMONES

Clownfish and sea anemones live together. A sea anemone has tentacles that sting most kinds of animals that come close to it. But it does not sting clownfish. The anemone protects clownfish from other fish that might want to eat them.

How many clownfish can you find on this page?

ANEMONES help protect clownfish, and clownfish help feed sea anemones. This kind of relationship is called symbiosis.

Can you say "symbiosis" (sim-bee-OH-sis)?

PORCUPINEFISH

Porcupinefish take big gulps of water to make themselves bigger. Most predators don't want to bite a big, prickly fish!

LIONFISH

Lionfish have spines filled with venom, which they use for protection. Lionfish are predators that usually hunt for food at night.

SURGEONFISH

Surgeonfish get their name from the sharp spines near the base of their tails that are similar to scalpels (sharp tools used by surgeons as part of their job).

PARROTFISH

Parrotfish have strong beaks that they use to eat coral. They are very colorful fish. Their color, shape, and pattern can change throughout their lives. They can also change between being male and female.

PUFFERFISH

Pufferfish, also known as blowfish, are strange, scaleless fish that can "puff" up to a much larger size. They're also very toxic!

Can you puff up like a pufferfish? Fill your cheeks with air, and try not to laugh. Remember to breathe when you need to!

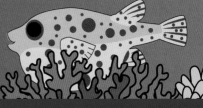

Like parrotfish, there are many sea creatures with another animal in their name. Can you think of any?

BOXFISH

Boxfish have a hard, boxy outer armor to protect themselves from predators. Some boxfish species also have horns and are known as cowfish!

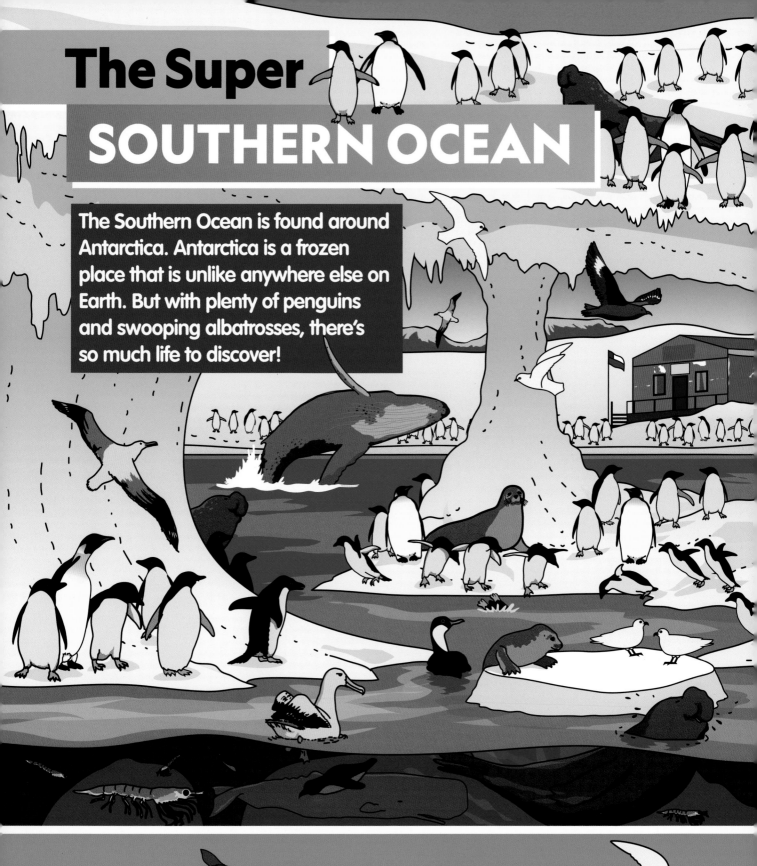

The Super SOUTHERN OCEAN

The Southern Ocean is found around Antarctica. Antarctica is a frozen place that is unlike anywhere else on Earth. But with plenty of penguins and swooping albatrosses, there's so much life to discover!

1 Sperm whale

2 Humpback whales

3 Weddell seals

4 Snow petrels

Did you know?

The coldest temperature on the planet was recorded here: -128 degrees Fahrenheit (-89°C)!

5 Wandering albatrosses

6 Southern elephant seals

7 Emperor penguins

8 Antarctic krill

EMPEROR PENGUIN

Emperor penguins are the world's largest penguins. They grow to 45 inches (115 cm)—about the same height as a six-year-old human. They gather in groups called colonies. The colonies are so big that they can be seen from space.

Can you waddle like a penguin from one side of the room to the other?

Blue whales eat lots of krill. What's your favorite food?

BLUE WHALES are the biggest animals on the planet! They have massive mouths with special filters that help them sieve their favorite food from the water.

WANDERING ALBATROSS

Wandering albatrosses are some of the biggest birds in the world, and they can fly nonstop! They can live as long as 50 years in the wild and have wingspans of over nine feet (3 m)!

If you could fly, where would you go and why?

SOUTHERN ELEPHANT SEAL

Southern elephant seals are the largest seals on Earth. They are called elephant seals because of their trunk-like snouts.

ANTARCTIC KRILL

Antarctic krill are like tiny little shrimp. They are one of the most important animals in the waters around Antarctica. This is because they are a food source for many animals that live there.

Can you think of any other creatures that jump out of the ocean?

HUMPBACK WHALE

Humpback whales do not actually have humps on their backs. They get their name from the way their backs arch when they jump out of the water just before they dive.

ADÉLIE PENGUINS are one of the smallest penguin species in Antarctica. When diving into water to find food, they can hold their breath for up to six minutes.

SPERM WHALE

Sperm whales have the biggest brains of any creature on the planet. When hunting, sperm whales dive so deep that they must hold their breath for about 90 minutes.

How long can you hold your breath? Remember to breathe if you feel dizzy!

WEDDELL SEAL

Weddell seals are born silver (their parents are gray). They can usually swim before they are two weeks old.

SNOW PETREL

Snow petrels are small birds—around the same size as a pigeon. They have pure white feathers, black eyes, and black beaks.

The Amazing
ATLANTIC OCEAN

The Atlantic Ocean is the second largest ocean in the world. It is surrounded by Europe, the Americas, and West Africa. Here you can find lots of sharks, dolphins, and octopuses.

Did you know?

Only around 5 percent of the world's oceans have been explored.

 **1 Great white shark**

 **2 Manatees**

3 Common octopuses

 **4 Marlins**

5 Thresher sharks

6 Hammerhead sharks

7 Swordfish

8 Bottlenose dolphins

THRESHER SHARK

Thresher sharks get their name from their large tails, which look like the long, hooklike blade on a threshing machine.

HAMMERHEAD SHARK

Can you guess how hammerhead sharks got their name?

Hammerhead sharks are great hunters. They have wide heads that give them a better range of sight compared to other sharks. Hammerhead sharks also use their heads to pin prey to the seafloor.

BOTTLENOSE DOLPHIN

Bottlenose dolphins are intelligent hunters. They are playful and fast, and swim in groups, working together to prey on schools of fish.

COMMON OCTOPUS

Common octopuses have large heads and eight arms! Each arm is covered in suckers. The suckers can be used to grip objects from the seafloor.

BASKING SHARKS feed near the surface. They look as though they are basking in the sun, which is how they got their name. Basking sharks have huge mouths that they use to filter food out of the water.

A great white shark can have up to 300 teeth! How many teeth do you have?

GREAT WHITE SHARK

Great white sharks are the largest hunting fish in the ocean. Their super sense of smell helps them detect blood from miles away.

How many types of shark can you name in 30 seconds?

SAILFISH are very fast swimmers. Their name comes from the crests that run the length of their bodies, which look like sails!

MANATEE

Manatees are large, gentle creatures also known as sea cows (though they are actually more closely related to elephants). They are very good at swimming and are graceful in the water.

SWORDFISH

Swordfish are large, quick hunters. Their famous swordlike snouts can be used to slash at their prey to stun them for quick and easy meals.

MARLIN

Marlins are some of the biggest and fastest fish in the sea. There are many different types of marlin, from massive black marlins to smaller white marlins.

Marlins can jump very high. How high can you jump?

The Icy
ARCTIC OCEAN

The Arctic Ocean is the world's most northerly ocean. It is also the smallest and coldest. Although small, its icy waters are packed with wildlife such as whales and walruses.

Did you know?

Climate change is warming the Arctic more than anywhere else on Earth.

1 Bowhead whale

2 Walruses

3 Narwhals

4 Beluga whales

5 Lion's mane jellyfish

6 Harp seals

7 Arctic cod

8 Arctic tern!

ARCTIC TERN

Arctic terns have the longest migration (movement from one area to another) of any animal. They fly from the Arctic to Antarctica and back again each year.

ARCTIC COD

Arctic cod are large fish that are common in Arctic waters. They have a substance in their blood that stops their bodies from freezing solid!

HARP SEAL

Harp seals don't spend much time on shore—they much prefer to swim. They can stay underwater for 15 minutes at a time.

LION'S MANE JELLYFISH

Why do you think it's called a jellyfish?

Lion's mane jellyfish are one of the largest jellyfish in the ocean. Their bodies can reach seven feet (2 m) in width, and their tentacles can stretch as long as 118 feet (36 m)—about the length of nine cars!

POLAR BEARS are the biggest land carnivores (meat-eaters) in the world. Their blubber (a layer of fat) and thick coat keep them warm in Arctic temperatures. Their fur also acts as excellent camouflage, helping them blend in with snow and ice.

NARWHAL

Narwhals are a kind of whale. The male narwhal has a single tusk that comes out of its head. Some females do, too. The tusks are filled with nerves that help narwhals detect changes in their environment.

Why do you think narwhals are called "unicorns of the sea"?

WALRUS

Walruses are huge! Both males and females have long tusks that they use to pull their big bodies out of the water. Walruses also use their tusks to break holes in the ice from below to help them breathe.

BOWHEAD WHALE

Bowhead whales are named after their massive bow-shaped mouths, which make them look as though they are smiling! Like powerful battering rams, they can smash through ice to make breathing holes.

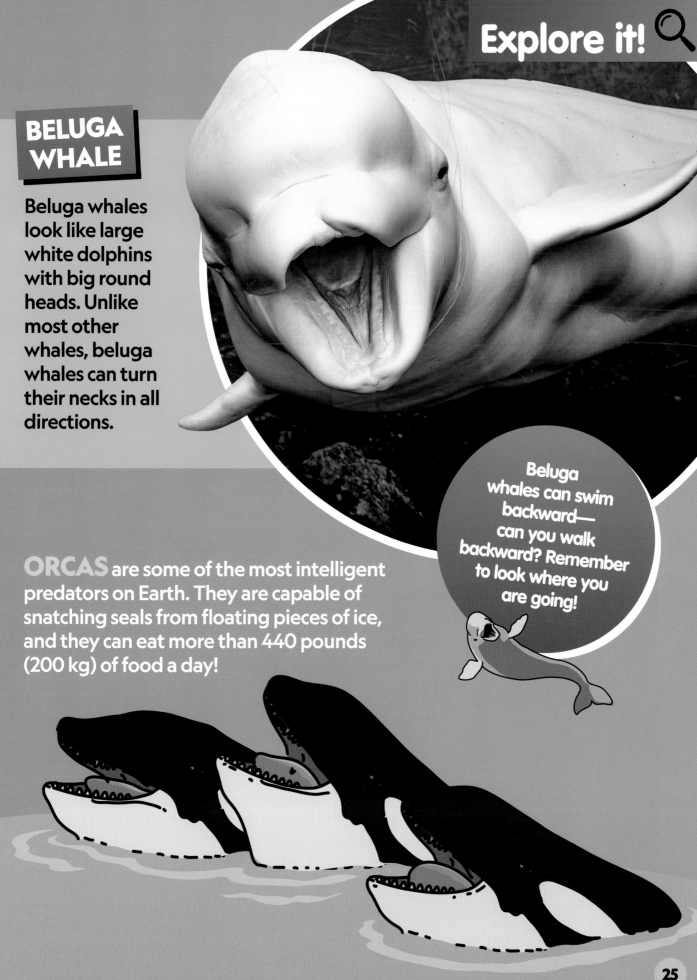

BELUGA WHALE

Beluga whales look like large white dolphins with big round heads. Unlike most other whales, beluga whales can turn their necks in all directions.

Beluga whales can swim backward—can you walk backward? Remember to look where you are going!

ORCAS are some of the most intelligent predators on Earth. They are capable of snatching seals from floating pieces of ice, and they can eat more than 440 pounds (200 kg) of food a day!

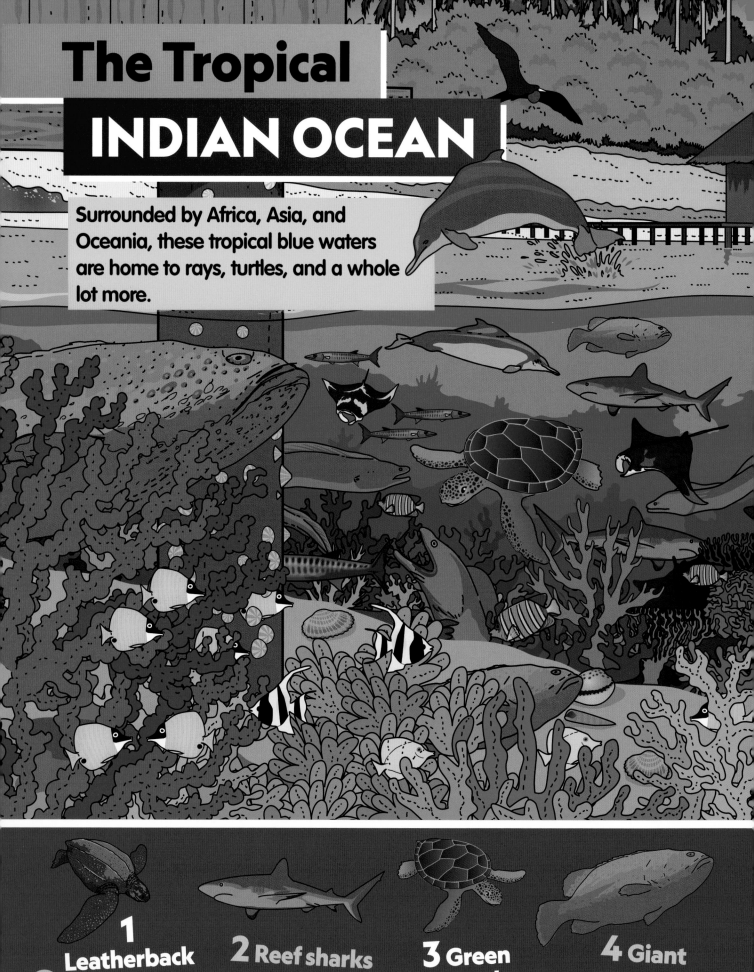

The Tropical INDIAN OCEAN

Surrounded by Africa, Asia, and Oceania, these tropical blue waters are home to rays, turtles, and a whole lot more.

1 Leatherback turtle

2 Reef sharks

3 Green sea turtles

4 Giant groupers

Did you know?

The Indian Ocean is the warmest ocean on Earth.

5 Manta rays

6 Indian Ocean humpback dolphins

7 Moray eels

8 Barracudas

27

MANTA RAY

Manta rays are the biggest species of ray. They have huge gaping mouths to gulp in plankton (the tiny ocean creatures they eat). Manta rays are nicknamed "devil fish" because they have horn-shaped fins on the top of their heads.

MORAY EEL

Moray eels are predators with long and often colorful bodies. Some species have toxic mucus (a slimy substance) covering their bodies. Their bite can be dangerous if a human gets too close.

BARRACUDA

Barracudas are speedy swimmers with torpedo-shaped bodies. Some of a barracuda's teeth point backward to stop any fish that tries to escape.

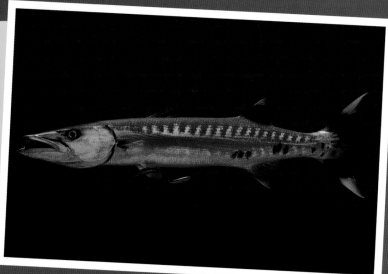

INDIAN OCEAN HUMPBACK DOLPHIN

The Indian Ocean humpback dolphin has a small triangle-shaped fin on its hump. These dolphins are endangered, meaning there are few left on the planet.

WHALE SHARKS are the biggest fish in the sea. They can reach up to 39 feet (12 m) long (about the length of three cars)! They are gentle giants and have even been known to let swimmers hitch a ride!

Whale sharks are huge! What's the biggest animal you've ever seen?

LEATHERBACK TURTLE

Leatherback turtles are the biggest turtles on Earth, weighing more than 11 adult humans! They have long flippers and are excellent swimmers. Their shells are made up of a leathery hide and small sheets of bone. This is why their shells look like they're made of leather.

Can you move like a turtle? Lie on the floor and try to cross the room using your arms and legs.

GIANT GROUPER

Giant groupers are massive bony fish that can weigh up to 880 pounds (400 kg). That's about the same weight as five adult humans!

GREEN SEA TURTLE

Green sea turtles are very large turtles. They can live as long as 100 years! Unlike land turtles, they cannot retract (draw back) into their shells.

REEF SHARK

Reef sharks are medium-size gray sharks that mainly eat small fish. They can smell injured and healthy fish and are very effective predators.

Look at all the sharks in this book. Which type is your favorite and why?

Exploring TIDE POOLS

Tide pools are pockets of water that are left behind on beaches when the tide goes out. Creatures like crabs and lobsters have adapted to life on land and in shallow water because of tide pools.

1 Lobster

2 Gobies

3 Oystercatchers

4 Hermit crabs

Did you know?

The force of gravity from the sun and moon creates tides.

5 Whelks

6 Urchins

7 Sea stars

8 Crabs

SEA STAR

Sea stars are strange animals that do not have brains or blood. They are invertebrates, which means they don't have backbones. They do have hundreds of tiny feet that allow them to slowly move around.

Stretch out your arms and legs really wide and make yourself into a human sea star.

LIMPETS are shelled creatures that grip tightly on to rocks. Some limpets will return to the same spot when the tide comes in. They do this because over time, their shells grow to fit the rock more tightly, keeping them from being swept out to sea.

Crabs walk sideways. Can you walk sideways around the room?

34

WHELK

Whelks are large sea snails found around the world. They have tall cone-shaped shells with wavy patterns.

URCHIN

Some sea urchins are very poisonous and have dangerous spikes poking out in all directions.

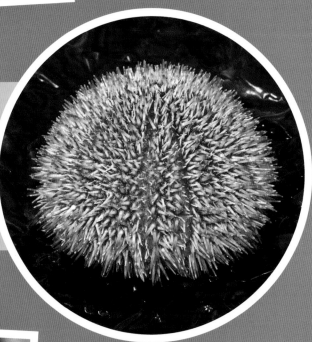

COMMON CRAB

Crabs are decapods, which means they have 10 feet. They sometimes shed these feet, but they are able to grow them back!

One type of hermit crab is all right-handed, and another is all left-handed. Try writing your name with the hand you don't usually use.

HERMIT CRAB

Hermit crabs are not actually crabs; they cannot form their own shells. Instead, they borrow shells from other animals—like whelks and other sea snails—or anything they can get their pincers on!

COMMON CUTTLEFISH can control how they float and what color they are. Baby cuttlefish use their tentacles to walk along the seafloor!

OYSTERCATCHER

Oystercatchers have long colorful beaks, which they use to open shellfish. They have white markings on their wings, which make them pretty easy to spot.

GOBY

Gobies are a type of small fish. In some species, when the female lays eggs, the male guards them very closely.

LOBSTER

Lobsters have long tails and big claws. They never stop growing. Lobsters are known for having long lives, with some species living for over 100 years.

Can you rearrange the letters below to make the name of another animal with claws?

B R A C

The DEEP OCEAN

There are many places in the ocean so deep that even light can't reach. Here, mysterious fish move about in the gloom. With parts of the ocean being so deep and difficult to explore, much of the ocean's mysteries are still waiting to be discovered.

1 Cookiecutter shark

2 Deep-sea viperfish

3 Sea cucumbers

4 Dumbo octopuses

Did you know?

The deepest known part of the ocean is called **Challenger Deep.** It is almost seven miles (11 km) below the surface.

5 Cusk eels

6 Fangtooths

7 Gulper eels

8 Deep-sea anglerfish

DEEP-SEA ANGLERFISH

Anglerfish have long needle-like teeth and very big mouths! Females also have fleshy bulbs that stick out over their heads to light up the dark waters. These bulbs attract small fish that are then swallowed up in one big bite!

DEEP-SEA HATCHETFISH

have strange-looking bodies that are shaped like a hatchet (a small axe).

Deep-sea hatchetfish have scrunched-up faces. What's the funniest face you can make?

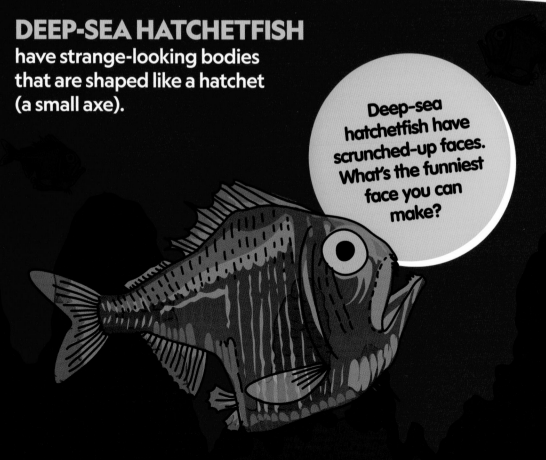

GULPER EEL

Gulper eels are long thin eels with mouths that look too big for their bodies. They swim with their mouths open to catch crabs and small shrimp.

CUSK EEL

Cusk eels are not true eels because they have fins just below their heads, called ventral fins. They also have whiskers that stick out from under their mouths to help them sense food.

FANGTOOTH

The fangtooth is an aggressive predator. Its fangs are so big, the fish is unable to fully close its mouth.

What is your favorite creature of the deep and why?

DUMBO OCTOPUS

Dumbo octopuses are little creatures that measure, on average, only 8 to 12 inches (20–30 cm) long. They're unique because they live deeper down than any other type of octopus and use their fins to move, rather than jets of water.

MEGAMOUTH SHARKS have huge jaws that they keep open while they swim along, letting food swim right into their mouths! Megamouth sharks are extremely rare, with very few ever seen in the wild.

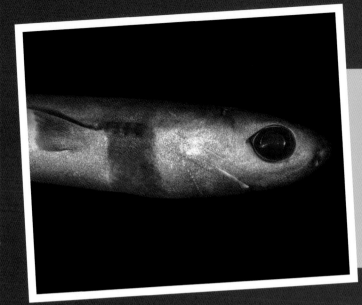

COOKIECUTTER SHARK

Cookiecutter sharks are small sharks, growing to around 20 inches (50 cm). They feed on larger animals by latching on to them and taking circle-shaped bites from their flesh.

DEEP-SEA VIPERFISH

Deep-sea viperfish are one of the most terrifying fish around! They use their massive teeth to pierce their prey, which they swallow whole.

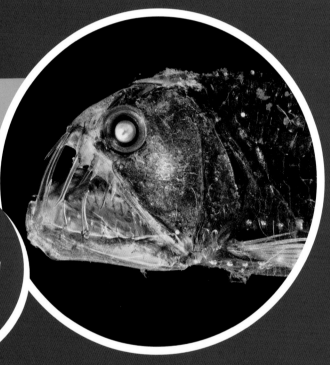

Can you push out your bottom jaw and make your best viperfish face?

SEA CUCUMBER

Sea cucumbers are like the ocean's answer to earthworms. They recycle waste and dead matter for smaller animals. Sea cucumbers that live in the deepest parts of the ocean have adapted to the darkness by lighting up!

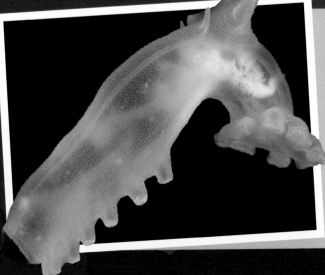

SOLUTIONS

The Precious Pacific Ocean

The Super Southern Ocean

The Amazing Atlantic Ocean

The Icy Arctic Ocean

The Tropical Indian Ocean

Exploring Tide Pools

The Deep Ocean

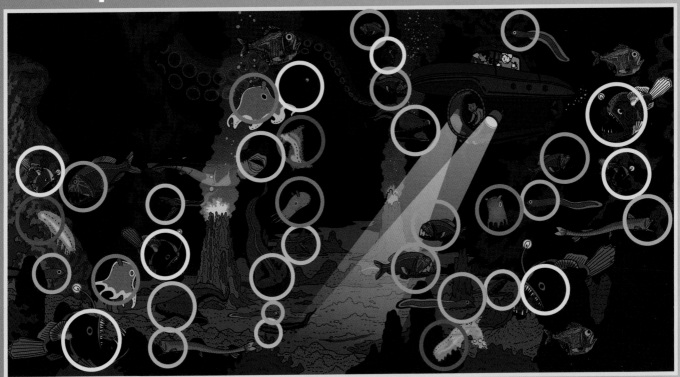

Where in the world can you find the places in this book? Check out the map below.

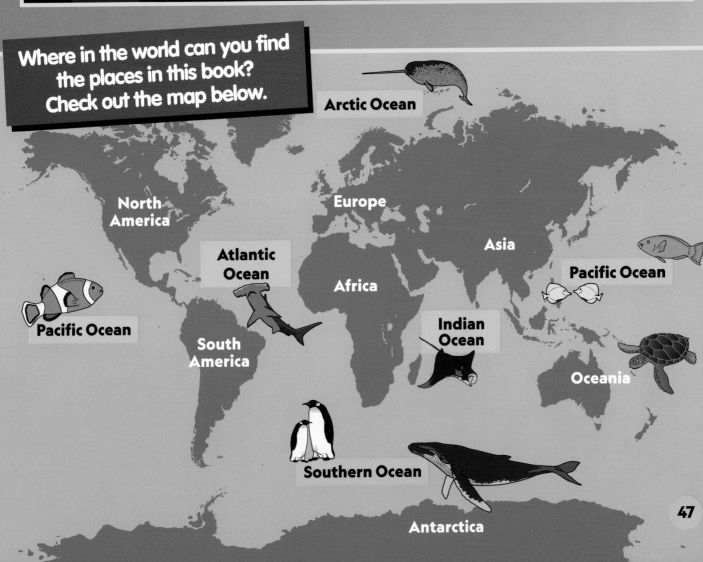

Arctic Ocean

North America

Europe

Asia

Atlantic Ocean

Pacific Ocean

Africa

Pacific Ocean

South America

Indian Ocean

Oceania

Southern Ocean

Antarctica